Even Now
the Embers

Critical praise for the books of Djelloul Marbrook

Artemisia's Wolf (title story in *A Warding Circle*)

...successfully blends humor and satire (and perhaps even a touch of magic realism) into its short length... an engrossing story, but what might strike the reader most throughout the book is its infusion of breathtaking poetry... a stunning rebuke to notoriously misogynist subcultures like the New York art scene, showing us just how hard it is for a young woman to be judged on her creative talent alone.

—Tommy Zurhellen, *Hudson River Valley Review*

Saraceno

...Djelloul Marbrook writes dialogue that not only entertains with an intoxicating clickety-clack, but also packs a truth about low-life mob culture *The Sopranos* only hints at. You can practically smell the anisette and filling-station coffee.

—Dan Baum, author of *Gun Guys* (2013), *Nine Lives: Mystery, Magic, Death and Life in New Orleans* (2009) and others

...a good ear for crackling dialogue... I love Marbrook's crude, raw music of the streets. The notes are authentic and on target...

—Sam Coale, *The Providence (RI) Journal*

...an entirely new variety of gangster tale... a Mafia story sculpted with the most refined of sensibilities from the clay of high art and philosophy... the kind of writer I take real pleasure in discovering... a mature artist whose rich body of work is finally coming to light.

—Brent Robison, editor, *Prima Materia*

Far from Algiers

...as succinct as most stanzas by Dickinson... an unusually mature, confidently composed first poetry collection.

—Susanna Roxman, *Prairie Schooner*

...brings together the energy of a young poet with the wisdom of long experience.

—Edward Hirsch, Guggenheim Foundation

Brushstrokes and Glances

Whether it is commentary on state power, corporate greed, or the intensely personal death of a loved one, Djelloul Marbrook is clear-sighted, eloquent, and precise. As the title of the collection suggests, he uses the lightest touch, a collection of fragments, brushstrokes and glances, to fashion poems that resonate with truth and honesty.

—Phil Constable, *New York Journal of Books*

Even Now the Embers

poems by

Djelloul Marbrook

LEAKY BOOT PRESS

Even Now the Embers
by Djelloul Marbrook

Acknowledgments

"North of trouble" was published in
Barrow Street, December 2009

First published in 2018 by
Leaky Boot Press
http://www.leakyboot.com

Copyright © 2018 Djelloul Marbrook
All rights reserved

No part of this book may be reproduced or transmitted in any form or by any means, electronic, mechanical, photocopying, recording, or otherwise, without prior written permission of the author.

ISBN: 978-1-909849-28-0

For Dr. Patricia Divine,
friend and light bearer

Contents

215 East 19th Street

215 East 19th Street	13
The bicycle	16
The eye in which we live	17
Your birthday	18
Something stuck	19
Providence, 1959	21
Hearing your hair grow	22
A bargain basement	23
Marabout's hawk	24
Old man slipping	25
New Year's Eve 2008	26
Doodling in my blood	27
Kill box	28
Burial instructions	29

Martini

Martini	33
In a cemetery	34
Under latex	35
Forgetful spy	36
Hiding Friday	37
Contraria	38
Sycamore and hydrant	39
Aeronaut in a poem	40
Absence	42
Facsimile	43
Your wardrobe	44
There I am after I've died	45

Shut my mouth	46
Dream me a little	47
Here	48
Morning reverie	49
Listen to the mockingbird	50
Sexton's song	51
Spring Street incident	52

North of trouble

Such plodding innocents	55
North of trouble	56
Define here	57
A certain park	58
Inside out	60
Eyesite	61
C4	62
The stare	63
Subways of the mind	64
In my disrespect	65
Pang	66
The question of torture	67
Try me in The Hague	68
Outage	69
Chance again	70
If I were an ant	71

The principle of optimal size

Holes	75
Summer thunder	76
The jar	77
Aught	78
The principle of optimal size	80
Shape	81
Firebreak	82
Rohypnol and the dead	83
Just a minute	84
Flower clock	85
Urushiol	86
Running under snow	87
Who is deceased?	88

Forlorn rest	89
The boundary brook	90
Up ahead	91
Smoke	92
Even now the embers	93

215 East 19th Street

215 East 19th Street

A hospital's there now
where nightmares hid in closets
and stairwells echoed *Vesti la giubba*

—I knew something like this would happen,
some kind of factory
making everything worse for us
than we could make for ourselves—

a hospital where I slept with polar bears,
Bengal tigers and snow leopards,
skinned and mothballed to be sure,
but certified to our dreams.

A taxidermy shop, an art studio,
mannikins, a shooting gallery,
benzine, carbon tetrachloride,
it's a wonder I'm still alive.

Cabrini Hospital now,
everybody's act scrubbed up.

Even cheetahs turned to rugs,
their sores and scars patched,
the silly fate of terrorists
not even guilty of dogma.

They were kinder to me in death,
theirs and mine, than parents;
I liked them better.

They had no quarrel with me,
not even that I'd been born.

They were wiser in their bins
than we who still had sex
and made telephone calls,
and they ranged farther
with nails in their hides,
stitched together with each other,
than we in our succumbings
to less than the day before.

No one, nothing dies.
That is my baseless claim
borne on eerie dusk
to an astronomy of dreams.

There's my grandma
at the top of the stairs;
we're not strangers
but we're not the same.
We have our places
in over-lives
richer than we imagined
and we sit
in such specificities—
yellow cups and saucers
wreathed in vines,
yellow lantern light
and a millbrook
rushing underfoot—
that no other place
seems real.

She died forty years ago
and I'm not sure this me's the one
she knew, but I know
morning intrudes
on what is going on.

And on, even when I think
time can be measured
and a sidelong glance
can make use of words.

Babylon's as viral in the air
as my latest excuse
for denying what I see.

Mary Corbett's lips
tasted like tomorrow.
Mary Corbett's lips
taste like tomorrow.
From her I learned
the playfulness of gods,
how dangerous it is to see them,
how deadly the taste of awe,
how first is last
and seasons after me
will taste of Mary
and no one else,
and somehow
I will testify
and someone will hear.

We don't want some people
or want them anywhere else,
don't want to know what happened here
or to us:
soiling of the mind,
scents of grief, acrid sorrows,
burnt sacrifice to the implacable
selfness of our bones,
the price of comfort paid:
all that is now an IV drip.

The bicycle

When I was eleven   I took my bike apart
My mother   whipped me with the chain
for the indignity   I had visited on the bike
and when I put it together again   working into the night
savoring the taste of blood   disks were left on the ground
It worked without them   as I have worked without
a few brake disks   a bolt or two
and a quarter pint short   of blood, brain lube and love

The eye in which we live

Here's how I think of growing up,
to take comfort in becoming dust,
unhurried, unhurrying, a friend
to the strewing of dandelions,
a star of microscopic firmaments
sending signals no one will see
except the eye in which we live.

Your birthday

Enough about you,
            Love, Mom.

Don't try to tell your story,
don't trade secrets away;
you're going to need it
to generate light.

What they didn't want to hear,
Mom and the other delusionals,
you need that to get there from here.

Don't let them tinker
or redact.
Your story's not an heirloom.
You can spin it all by yourself,
but only you know where you hid
the truth, your ticket
to the crystal ship
nobody will ever see but you.

Lots of luck with this project,
your amazing grace;
the rest is a birthday card.

Something stuck

I'm misheard a lot
asked to repeat myself
I know the reason
I'm disquieting
because I'd look
as if I saw
even if I couldn't see

I'm seen too much
but not seen well
I know the reason
I seem about to say
seem intent to say
words you'd kill
not to hear

misheard, misread
something stuck
in a crack in my brain
is how I got this way
is what things play to
and I'm not sure
the pain's exorbitant

study the wall
over my shoulder
greet the person
behind me

precisely because
I don't disappear
I'm on to us

Providence, 1959

Pour these memories into my head,
pretend there is a purpose,
trouble the sleep of the dead:
Frank Cahill's gutted nose,
the hole in Armin Meisner's heart,
battered Judy at our project door,
and bloody-handed Amy.
Children raising children—
did God help us all
in the rain of Providence,
help us who helped ourselves
to Narragansett beer,
post-partum grief and cumshaw parts
for our jalopies?
God bless the Salvation Army
for clothes and furniture
and the Navy for my see-ya pay—
pour these memories into my grave,
stir them with piss on a wintry day
and watch me rise and blow away.

Hearing your hair grow

Some nights when the air is a nausea of thoughts
I think back wistfully to the day before we met.
I am the bother you chose for yourself,
fly in your skull those electric nights.
Whoever you waste time waiting for to die
is already a ghost in your head,
someone, I hope, who hears your hair grow
from another continent, someone who knows
how disappointed you are that it matters.
You know you don't mean some people well
but you know they'll be watching you
for the rest of your life and certain things you do
are to spite them when nobody
cares about them but you. It isn't hell,
not yet, but it's the craziness you need
to get there, and along the way it's your contempt
for what you chose. I didn't want to be
your demon or your angel, but I hear you breathing
as if the moment we met still mattered.

A bargain basement

Even angels have their price.
I would have settled for Wonder Woman
or a knock-off of her bracelet,
but this guy wanted my name.
Can you imagine that, my good name?
What a bogus protest I put up!
My name for protection, what a deal!
What the hell did I need it for?
Nobody could pronounce or spell it.
What did I need any name for?
I'd just be me and he'd be an angel-mook
with a borrowed name,
                    so who got raped?
We'd talk about it again in fifty years
after drunkenness and sobriety
and other near-death experiences,
talk about it to hell and gone,
talk about angels with a terrorist's name,
talk about how your face comes off
with masks until you can't remember
your face when you gave up your name
to have a friend in this friendless place.

Marabout's hawk

What is this stern desert face
doing in this month of sundaes?
Are these the sherbet times the sheik
promised us drugged assassins
or am I a stone in this moraine
mourning some lost glacier?
When my belly hurts I don't care.
I think I am a marabout's hawk,
but the old fool didn't train me well.
I'll plop his eye in his young wife's lap
and resign these unheard of bones
to the pick-a-stick of arctic wolves.

Old man slipping

I know where things used to be,
I know such people used to bore me.
I forget where objects come from;
is this a good or a bad thing?
I look at them with wolves' eyes;
my enemy is ownership.
If these objects are commercials
I am slipping uninterruptedly
beyond hucksters' reach,
beyond those con men courted
because so much had been withheld.
All this good and bad forgetting,
remembering at inappropriate times,
has earned me reflux disease
and better sight through cataracts
than I saw through love or ambition.
I see that what I didn't want to see
is the nth-heartedness of the boy
who stared the ghouls to death.
Now drenched in ancient light
I butt the plate-glass future
with the grin of a man who's shot
the cable news with a twelve gauge
propped between his knobby toes.

New Year's Eve 2008

everyone has to party
and die of cancer
because looking away
is easier than seeing
where there is no will

what're you looking at
my mother used to say
when I was looking well
at any number of things
that didn't bear scrutiny

what're we looking at
when we'd rather die
than look at how we live
is what I used to say
before I fell asleep

and slept a bit too long
and woke up less wise
than when I'd been a boy
but somewhat better able
to express bafflement

Doodling in my blood

There's always a bad connection
with the one whose signals you ignore
when you decide to waste your time.

Static, fade-outs and breaks
are your desert for folding up
your superior antennae,

but if you let the phone ring on the last day
you can redeem even the coupons
of possibilities that went bankrupt.

The urgency of the ring is bogus;
everything happens the eleventh hour,
i.e. the splendor of not kidding yourself again.

The disconnects that amuse me in old age
once seemed to hold my life in their hands.
Now they remind me of Voltaire's smile.

They trifled with my wounds. I knew it.
But I hoped to make them benefactors
and nurses. They doodled in my blood.

This is my log entry to you whom I leave
to wrap things up, to pretend to be me
while I move on to find us a new place to live.

Kill box

When I turn in this name
will I chuck it in a box
for meltdown and recycling
or will I hand it back
to its rightful owner?
What if I don't like him
or he spits in my eye,
who will I be to care?
There should be a kill box
for words we abused,
names that didn't fit
and a warm embrace
of silence settling in.

Burial instructions

Everybody ends up somewhere
      and I can't think of anywhere
            that would seem probable.

Nothing ever seems likely
      except being in the wrong place
            under watchful eyes.

So you can't bury me here
      without some stupid debate
            about where here is.

There won't work either,
      being light years away
            from my enemies' imagining.

Ash is good. I don't want
      a grave you can ignore
            or come and shit on.

Martini

Martini

Cash registers had their humidors;
who could have envisioned this—
words thickening the air,
a life's work distorted in a wink
and distinction dissolved
between thief and fanatic?

We can hardly digest our youth
much less inhabit this cyclotron.
Cash registers had their humidors
when life stirred in an alembic,
but into this weirdly broken gin
the bartender drops a cherry.

In a cemetery

not in the ground not yet but in my head
where I honor you no less than gods
                                          rest in motion
and then we will in someone else's head
                                          rest in motion
stars conjuring beasts beasts weaving
participles of time together rest
not in the ground not yet but here
where the beasts drift in and out rest
assured that I have not forgotten you
and if there is an ever never will

Under latex

What I've touched dawdles on my fingers,
soon it may be known whom I've touched.
And as for traces of my mind, my image,
circled as in Skip to My Lou by the moods
of many irises, looks out upon the world
with the sorrow of a slave and defies
the grim clinicians to show my imprint
on the crimes and motives at hand.

No intent hides under latex, no influence
is bleached away: we're the sum of the march
from the jungle or another planet, and if
I may steal from the lips of dogmatists,
that is the most intelligent design—
that our ineradicable encounters say
no one can be cut out from the circle:
we are inescapably each other's darlings.

Forgetful spy

Today I forgot to wear my face.
At ten I thought it fatal in a spy.
At noon I disappeared in windows
and knew the worst was over.
I had resumed my permanent state.

It was the morning I'd come here for.
At home they would be pleased,
lovers of no gender or person.
It's only because we have faces,
disguises, that we need a home.

Hiding Friday

I never lose days, I hide them
in the glances of strangers
and find them in scatterings
of dreams across the night.

A lost day causes no panic;
I may not know where I put it,
but my dreams will not conspire
to give me bad directions.

One look over a deli counter
may be more valuable than blood,
but diamonds are no good
if you don't know how to cut them.

Contraria

Love, murder, incest brush by,
fragrances most of us can't follow,
leaving rooms redolent, us unfulfilled.

I know nothing in which I'm not complicit;
shouldn't I be enjoying it?
Foreignness is the greatest lie.

We flower and smell of type,
exert our intellect to belie it
and look over the shoulders of our angels.

Sycamore and hydrant

If we had the noses of dogs on 57th street
we'd have shorter, more exciting lives.

We'd leave our markers with aplomb
instead of pretending we don't have any.

Our pretensions would be insupportable
and would crash as regularly as the markets.

We would always know where we've been
and we'd know where you'd been too.

We'd be hard-wired to our memories,
and we wouldn't think of editing them.

But the standing rebuke of sycamores
compared to the hominess of hydrants,

the tyranny of always being pulled away
might outweigh our fragrant pleasures,

and yet what is society but a leash
in a world where all the scents are faint?

Aeronaut in a poem

He is more in danger in a poem,
especially his own, than a mite in a clock,
and less likely to get out alive

because a poem is never what it seems to be,
nor is a dream, and in this dream
his poem is a gold and Carrara city

in which he doesn't speak the language
and as a foreigner studying a foreign self
brings microbic diligence to the work.

The city's caprices and whimsies frustrate him.
His lift-offs feel lead-footed. Without his shoes
he worries about touching things.

At least, he reassures himself, I'm not sewn into my own skin
but have managed to dehisce and drop
my dusky ether robe

to explore the reaches of the city
as the supple number aught
and not a brittle numeral or two.

Oh please, give me a break, he tells himself.
I am this hieratic me only when waiting for a part
for my shit-detectors. Get over yourself.

Who, granted grace of number, need be understood?
He could be a falcon or a rat and maybe
he had become an angel without warning.

No one notices his nakedness
or minds his yammer. Foreigners talk to themselves.
Art once made is alien. Those reaches

of which he spoke?— a kind of daring
to which the artist never quite catches up.
He remains a visitor to his own mind.

Who let him in? His papers are out of order.
He has no skills of use to this city-state.
He'll be a burden, no stoop labor here.

Jump! the crowd yells as crowds do,
what do crowds know about strangers?
He blinks at immaculate ratchets and faces

and cuts his fingers on their edges
as if it were his work, a profession even.
He understands the brutishness of crowds.

He swears to immigration, swears up and down
that if they would kindly deport him
he would write no more poems. He's lying,

they like the lie. It seems to bode well
for future relations, which they're bound to have
if he can't get a good night's sleep.

Absence

No one cares for me without you,   I'm an empty seat.
My small claim to life   is that I studied you
as hard as I could   and in that way acquired
a human semblance.   In your absence it falls off.
I lope and howl   in the fey light.

Facsimile

So these memories, did they come back?
I think I will go bike on ice.

That scar on your forehead, how did you get it?
Haven't you noticed I'm a cyborg?

And what about that umbrella on a sunny day?
It's for sticking in messengers' spokes.

Did you ever hear azaleas bark
or encounter Artemis in a snit?

Her dogs are nothing but your memories,
so if you forget how to tie your shoes,

consider it a small price to pay
for the sound of gnashing teeth you've forgotten.

When I short out as I often do
and everyone grows an extra five feet,

when I'd rather kill than hear children squeal
I remember the odor of certain people

and their smiling little crimes
that killed me in my bed, and yet I must account

for the behavior of this facsimile
whom people swear looks like me.

Your wardrobe

I dress in ancient light,　　I bequeath my own ahead.
Earth barely plugs a sunspot.　　We stir cosmos in a pore.
Look out into the past　　and when your light arrives
you will have lived other lives　　while always rushing away
from illusion called today.　　We are mostly empty space
and so each magnetic face　　enraptures us with the glow
of fires lit a million years ago.　　Who will wear my light,
my transit of collisions　　in the cities that arise
from my sea of dreams,　　who will almost remember?

There I am after I've died

No sealant for these nerve ends,
their mouths frozen screams—
every kind of warning buzzes in.
This is the vigilance of the child
who tucks his murdered spirit
in his bed and lurches on,
a contraption of himself.
Tell fortunes with my bones,
they know how to spell,
but these rioting ganglia shake
their fists at faceless police.
There I am after I've died,
waiting in unfamiliar chairs
in an airport without planes
breathing a well-remembered breath
when underfoot of Amazons I saw
a crystal ship and knew
history would turn against them.
Rest, my face, and I will live
my other life behind you,
the one read to me in dreams
in a voice very like my own.
Time is torn on measured thorns—
I could not have lived
in England sixty years ago,
and yet I know I did and do
and expect to finish that life out
in garlands woven here.

Shut my mouth

I don't work rooms, they work me.
Gargoyles arrive early
to perch on shoulders
and shelves and shut
my mouth with mockery.

Crowded rooms remind me
things could be worse
but not much. Demons
promise we'll be friends
but doubts await them—
mad puppets in their closets.

I prefer hubbub to words.
I surf rollers over heads
out the window to a beach
where a few survivors rest
from weathering each other.

Dream me a little

I didn't even like the dog,
the people were obnoxious, I was obsequious,
and by the time I figured out it was a dream
the only thing I could do was wake up.

The boss was feeling me up
but I couldn't remember my sex.
I was so upset as I made them drinks
I forgot to spit in them.

Come to Hollywood with us, he said.
I've never been west of anything myself:
can you believe I said that?
The dog was rolling on the floor.

I must have wanted something;
is that going to be my story,
I must have wanted something
a little like someone's death.

Here

I don't know where here is
and yet abut people who do.
Sextant and SatNav won't help
because here is having a place.

Here be myth and water
and dragons waiting
to sting and eat us:
comic certainties.

Here is walking in wet cement,
a fire-setting fireman,
a bribe-taking cop:
here's to never being here,

and there, for that matter,
is not such a desirable place,
implying as it does
setting out from here.

Morning reverie

Problems come faster than light,
leave chocolates on their beds,
hang up don't-disturb signs,
remember to tip the maid.

This is a crime scene
even if you haven't decided
which crime to commit;
your little detective bots

will be turning it inside out
and handing evidentiary tidbits
to your prosecutorial friends
who will bore holes in your head

pouring their disappointments
into those unused caverns
where your vast potential
glitters and grins in the dark.

Listen to the mockingbird

Are we categorical to birds?
Bully jays, burgling cardinals?
And what do porpoises make
of all our flopping around?
I know red-tailed hawks
think we lack concentration

and we're crashing bores
to great blue herons.
Dogs seem less judgmental,
but does it serve them well?
Everything must be pigeonholed
or we'd become amnesiacs.

Buzzards are no problem,
we're already roadkill,
and we know how we look
to the circling hawk.
We've got birds so well pegged
it would worry us

if we had common sense,
but we haven't noticed
nothing stays in its place,
nothing we've got figured,
and yet our daft response
is to build more pigeonholes.

Sexton's song

The organ cracks the church to crumbs.
It is too big and costs too much.
Hallelujah, welcome, money bags.

Someone's always too big for the place
and always costs too much; something
always prompts too much praise and joy.

All those right-angle cracks in the walls
are the costs of trumpets and triumphs:
lift your voices and paint them over.

I wait for grand dames to fart at the rail
because nothing is as obscene
as our hatred of the Jews

in the name of our lord you know who.
I wish there were another place to go,
but I'm old and I've been here too long.

Spring Street incident

I know exactly how you feel,
to hell with your right to feel it.
I hear the angel at your ear,
may she walk against the light.

I know exactly what you see,
I will convince you otherwise.
I see your angel point at me,
I will break her little finger off.

So it is between us, you and me,
everyone, false positives,
sciences of what not to see:
the holy of holies is pretense.

You know what I'm up to,
the work-around starts from there.
I know how you feel about it,
I offer your angel a settlement,

but in the course of the negotiation
we die, and a turbaned taxi driver
notices two bag ladies scampering
to pick up chimeras in the street.

North of trouble

Such plodding innocents

Connecting the dots from A to C
he misses B and calls it a shortcut.
I'd take heart if it were like synapses
going around a few burned-out cells,
but I think it's more like political spin.

Some might say passive aggression,
but whatever it is, I worry about B
spinning out and crashing on the lawn,
an unknown object sizzling in the grass,
shorting circuits in my head.

Maybe he can get from here to there
but just not like most of us do
or maybe sheer delight in snubbing B
suggests a world of getting over on
such plodding innocents as me.

North of trouble

always sailing somedamnwhere in my sleep
snow-blind between two continents
in a Redningskoite not a felucca or zarook
or J-boat or anything elegant
                                        sailing
north of foul breath and particular trouble
I scan the gale for growlers
breaching whales and broaching subjects
such as where I've been and what I mean
by skedaddling in a backyard boat
in the middle of the night with no intention
of dealing with another day
                                      and then
a hand picks up the boat and puts it down
in a scale model of my bedroom
where a few things are disarranged as if
the jolly boat
                              Captain Mayhem at the helm
made a course correction and put in
to a cove described to him before
to wait out the inquisition of the sun

Define here

Sex is the price of doing business here.
Should one electric shudder shut
the secret elven door in my head
I'd be a stateless person, a ghoul
with a passable face, a man
bereft of being a hairless otherling.

I don't say it's too high a price,
I'm not an anti-tax nincompoop,
but it's a death of one kind or another
and we never rise on its morning side
the way we went to bed, and not least
of what we lose is loss's measure.

What's a little electrocution
in the name of public order
whether by lightning or by sex,
a little shock therapy for one
rattled by too many recognitions,
a restoration of the blotto state

for someone else's peace of mind?
I'm talking to you about high taxation,
about not getting off cheap (hah hah);
I'm talking to you about the veil of illusion
between the world you think is yours
and the worlds between the cracks.

A certain park

In the vast uptowns of my dreams
it is always Sunday morning,
the sun is eating away mottoes
incised on ludicrous homes.
Errol Flynn is jogging
with murderous intent.
I must get to a certain park.
Panic hides directions from me.
I need a bicycle; the trolley stops
in the wrong neighborhoods.
You'd think I'd left the right ones
but that's the nature of panic:
I have never lived anywhere
and in these mausoleums
are no kitchens or bathrooms,
no need of recognitions,
only the antiseptic light
of those I was born to importune.

Something of inestimable value
awaits me in that park, a life
I lived and lost before its time,
a farewell never quite said,
remembered in elevators
that skip the floors where anyone
I might have known lives,
memories swept up in lobbies
by officious handymen.

My chances of getting there
are about as good as Monday.
What kind of week should begin,
what stranger to tell me that?
Who is not strange in this uptown,
stranger, that is, than me? Who
is not a memory too tattered
by a constant wind to materialize?
My feet no longer hit the ground.

Inside out

As usual there will be Nazis,
feldgrau like a month of rain.

No one of high purpose gets through,
everyone forgets where they're going.

How will the usual Nazis feed us
our gruel and crust of grief

and we entrust safety to them
chagrined it's only them we fear?

Each inside has an out; row on row
Nazis are making sure it's so.

Eyesite

If I had a black armchair
I wouldn't put a red pillow in it.
Maybe turquoise or white.
Now, if I knew that about you
you'd be sure to sit elsewhere.

If I had a black sloop
I wouldn't set white sails.
Maybe burgundy or blue.
Now, if you knew that about me
would it make your pupils cringe?

What we ignore at our peril
defines us, sloops and chairs,
and what's good for us
rarely opens our pupils up,
leaving us to twinkle in the dark.

If I had a naked thought
(remember when you had nothing but)
I'd let you in to rummage
and rearrange my belongings,
but could you take your quibbles off?

C4

Funny how our minds stick
in places our bodies quit,
beds now rats' nests,
rooms molded black and burned,
broken dolls in attics,
true fuses of our sex—
we're not wholly here
or anywhere but there.

When the bridge falls
torpors drown us.

Or did we stock C4
in a charring boat
on a floorless sea
and sweat to bring
her to a hasty port
against sumatras
of ordinariness?

The fuse of sex is minded
by our demons & our angels
and we must go talk to them
on the rotting bridge
over the roiling sea
should love now come to be.

The stare

Everyone imagines his own hell;
mine is having to watch the credits.
Done with that, time for the film to begin.
None of the parts or off-screen jobs
appealed to me. I preferred to be the screen,
and the only thing I take with me
is the whiteout for which I was subtly chosen.
In me they could begin again, rubbing
off their ills and agues on my dismay,
projecting one and then another until
a character they liked appeared, leaving
me in rubbish bins, ditches, lurches,
all the places memories soil. Endless lists
of credits, misused music, bad typography
have hardly sufficed to make a life,
but I've managed to live one between them
knowing all along I should have been allowed
to see the picture first, and would have been
                                    had I not so fixed a stare.

Subways of the mind

Oh yes, that first despairing glance,
plea to heaven for surcease from me,
screeches and rattles along its track
to this midnight station sixty years later,
discharging malign doubts that scurry
to the wormholes of commiserators.

Every look comes hurtling underground
freighted with its former circumstance;
our days are stations where we wait
for those moments to emerge and grind
to a halt at our feet. The doors fly open
and the histories of hurt break out.

The subway system of the mind inflicts
schedule changes and whimsies at will.
Its stations are poorly lit and menacing
depending on where you started from.
If you pushed the stiles in love depend
on clean and well lit cars and friendly faces,

but if the stiles are one more molestation
darkened cars will shove their corpses
in your face, at every station rapists wait,
and all who found you inconvenient
for even looking as if you would despair
pour themselves out into your head.

In my disrespect

Crows' caw, roses' red, lilacs' scent
betray the civic order, barge,
insist, foment anarchy, part
the anchor rode of sanity.

There is no pity in the sudden,
but we don't live in other species' time;
in their own millennia dandelions
deal me one psychotic morning.

I am afraid of the certainty
of objects, the animations
of those who come up behind me,
ambushes in the thickets of my head.

It is only in my disrespect
for other forms of life that I impute
to their insistence my craziness.
Each to each, this is the bite

and pheromone of foreignness.
Driving so much and many out,
our minds have followed suit:
and now each beauty disembowels.

Pang

if I offer you help
and you say stuff it
I understand that better than love

and if you would be God
dealing me my just deserts
reject my love

you will never know
when I take my power back
but it will pang your bones

The question of torture

I aspire to be a person of interest
and to approve of torture
on religious grounds;
in this way I hope to belong
to the washed elite, the baptized;

all death is going to be for me
is the end of my quest for something to quit,
or perhaps a re-examination
of my sense of humor,
perhaps the award of a golden windmill.

We'll see. Or not. In the meantime
I suggest we torture our enemies
with sermons and cartoon beliefs,
and if they had any sense
they'd drive us mad with theirs.

Try me in The Hague

If the purpose of a picture
is to leave nothing to be said
try me in The Hague
for every syllable.

What is more heinous
than one word too many?

Poets and artists get along
when they do because
they understand reticence.

A comma in the wrong place
or an unnecessary one
is an offense punishable
by fame and the horrors
of the church
or any other club.

I like the line not drawn,
the word not said, the fillip
resisted more than God
or motherhood, serving
as they do to define God
as ably as empty space.

Outage

The young man recedes.
We go in up to our armpits
but can't pull him out of himself
and if we did he'd be inside out:
we'd be responsible
for his exposure to viruses,
so we must leave him hanging there,
a traffic light in a power outage,
and leave that dead village, too,
as fast as rubber wheels and diligence
allow under circumstances
which have become foreign to us.
He only looks as if he should
tell us the rules. This is how we go out
when someone is waiting
to go on or turn.
This sad boy is our worst instinct,
death rehearsed in an acrid town
in high winds and the sound
of metal mocking thunder.

Chance again

You have to do something
about some people in the street,
smile or block their way, then wonder why.

Somebody wants your seat
not because it's theirs
but because you exist, woeful you.

Someone's disturbing glance
reflects your own and a curse
blossoms in the night.

You unsettle both of you,
a dangerous bond
that could lead to marriage

or war or hot pursuit
through a dozen lives,
and trying to shrug it off

imperils the ordinary course
of your blood and sense of time:
you blew that chance again.

If I were an ant

I don't think humans bear the scrutiny
that insects do, but if I were an ant
I might have a better opinion of humans
or not. Our faces under lens appall
and cosmetics present another species
unlike the one we clothe. Television,
so concerned with our anxieties
and what may result in death,
lets slip that money makes us garish.

There is in us so much to rouge and fix,
to cover and reveal we need comics
to remind us we were born gods
and for the rest of our lives succumb
to base persuasion and being haunted
by powers that we came here to use
and gave up to comfort parents.
No wonder inquiring looks can cause
havoc in churches, streets and bedrooms.

The principle of optimal size

Holes

Nothing's holier than holes;
how else do light & penetration
move us to go or see or believe
in another side of things?
So then what's holy is not there
but is the socket of an eye intent
to hold an orb that is much like

heavenly bodies orbiting.
The holes in stories are news.
Pinholes in canvas prove
artists do not mean to belie
worlds in back of art.
Which, what, who, where—
we're fit to abandon totems

in favor of our better selves,
thinner than thin air, prepared
for the holiness that hints
of divine black emptiness
that cajoles us to explode
and throw our light ahead
to the reaches of imagining.

Summer thunder

Tornado light, El Greco skies,
what am I ready for?
Ozone recklessness,
undersides of leaves
and cryptics belie
we ignore each other.
Let this night loosen

our dread shapedness,
electrify our minds
with awe of borrowedness.
I can't read by this light
anything but my remaking
in the images of creatures
who touch my hair and breathe

on my eyelids while I sleep.
Paint with clouds tonight,
pour faerie blood in cracks
between this illusion and the next,
show me an afterimage
of where I lived before
this lewd and tinkered life.

The jar

A word in a jar of words,
I stir on a sill in the sun.
What am I becoming,
how reduced to one?
Are we seeds to sprout in water,
minerals at a mazurka?
I'm no genie in a bottle
conniving to get out.
I'm content to dream. I vote
as my secrets cook
to welcome what I become.

Aught

One is that one word that lops off
dicks of fools, heads of saints;
it doesn't belong to anyone
and for our desire to own it
it wears us like a drop of water,
which, it now turns out,
has a memory.

One is impenetrable.
Not even mathematicians
may claim to have slept with it
and those of us who touch it
touch it when we're least ready
to touch anyone or be touched.

One might look like entrapment
in two dimensions but not
considering it rode the preceding here
and opens all that follows.

Therefore nothing is more frightening
than one which ought to convey
everything as well as naught.

The dark other would have to bear
one to us, since no friend would,
and yet far from thank the Arabs
we'd rather count their dead.

We are looking for the one
as if there were something to contain,
looking to be encircled,
or you could say ensorcelled,
as if by drawing one is meant
others are looking in.

The principle of optimal size

If that's about the size of it
better ask if it's the right size,
perfect scale and volume
the promise of physics,
elegance of calculus:
an optimum for each of us,
agnostics to ideologues,
particles to gas giants,
one size at which our genes
and grand designs perform
consonant with hidden whim.

If this were the size of it, then,
we might perceive war as junk.

Shape

Lust, my Cubist mind, to free
faces from their appurtenances,
give emeralds back to earth,
conceits to their geometries,
make less of that imaginary more
that holds us hostage to parents
and blinds our eyes with gnats.

I know which earrings throw a fit
on squarish heads, which fingers
ought to tap instead of paint.
I know the rights of Braque and Gris,
bare canvas rites of Cézanne.
I trace the littoral between undress
and the holy lustiness of shape.

Firebreak

What if it was a controlled burn
but I callowly called it uncontrolled?
What if adultery, drunkeness and divorce
were not crown fires and conflagrations
but a reasoning in kilns
carefully laid out by the idea of Apollo
if not the god himself, a ritual
for a pyrotechnic life in a place
only a crystal ship could reach?
What if meltdowns and despair
were firebreaks and I needed to divest
devil's walking sticks and sweet gum,
forestall understories that sap
coniferal prayer and aspiration?
I could not have been the engineer.

Rohypnol and the dead

Assume the dead are watching us.
Drop sequined hypocrisy, shame
and pretense on the bedroom floor,
dance with them before the mirror,
let the walls whirl and time see-saw.

Have they got it in for us? In what?
In what part of our creatureliness
are they invested? And as for them,
the ones we wanted and wanted to kill,
let us celebrate our nakedness

even if we only pretend they see us
in our showers and utmost throes,
otherwise our shame is most of use
to those who wish to swindle us.
Let us get off the minute hand

and follow their pheromones back
to what we wanted of them when
we were so chemically deranged.
Come, you shameful, to a wicked party
where inhibitions are Rohypnol.

Just a minute

Considering hinges and linchpins,
everything happens in a minute,
that minute we stretch into novels,
celebrate and loathe, examine
and in so doing shut our eyes
to what embraces or engulfs us.

If I stamp and shrug the minute off
I might as well wear a plastic shroud,
crash through streets and cemeteries
and finally be stopped by a forty-five
because I couldn't bear a single moment
enduring miracles under my nose.

Flower clock

I like the way some anger doubles back
taking schmoozers by surprise.
I love the ballerina who forgets
to hand her partner a rose,
so happy is she in herself.
Why should they think of us?
Who are we compared to blossom's
fuse and someone else's timing?

Urushiol

What about love is urushiol,
sunken fang and regret?

Snakes need scales to slither,
do we slither by hate to love,

refusing to revere the ones
we hanker for, pit vipers

poked by our discontents?
What is there in love to strike,

in its dangers to destroy?
Isn't it a familiar nest

and toiling of the gods,
a divine enwrithement?

Running under snow

If it had been a silicon life
would I have smiled at peril
like a lunatic in the mirror,
would I have let two whores
stroke me with straight razors,
dipped Cohibas in Calvados
and looked so hard for trouble?
Does carbon have to do with sense?
I put so little in any of it,
this life running under snow,
how is there some of me to wonder
if there is intelligent life
in anything that bears a name?

Who is deceased?

She has a notion to dig him up,
for he had been loved by elementals.
She has an urge to dig him up,
but will he be there? She doesn't think so,
he hadn't been here. But his eyes,
they remain everywhere and that,
she knows, doesn't hold much promise
for him resting in a hole just because
a stranger casually called him dead.
There are certain ones we should exhume
to see which world we live in.
But how to dig him up, and what if
he isn't there, if her obsession turns out
to be the sensibility she will need
to live in the world she suspects this is?
She sees the question of digging him up
is whether we like our suspicions better
than where our courage might lead.
Whether she does or doesn't want to dig him up
the elementals will keep on loving us
and we will keep on loving to be afraid.

Forlorn rest

What am I determined to hurry today,
what words to burn for warmth,
grievances to serve this end?

Who hankers for this pearl in me,
hard teardrop of disbelief
that when I summon someone comes?

I would rest in the arms of angels
if I were the sort of person who could rest
not knowing if they were alabaster.

The boundary brook

What I want from your face
that can't be had from any other,
isn't it what God wants of mine?
What's history but how we turn away?
May I not be a boundary brook
between heaven and earth,
you and me, a filament
of smoke. What I see
in your face is the map
of where I've been.

Up ahead

Now is much too soon for me,
I can't catch up with what is happening.
Where is my moment's grace?
The moment up ahead brushed me aside;
I hear it in my ear, smell it on my skin.
No, do not look back to see me stunned.
Go on, I must finger the beads. It's sad
to be ambushed by the slightest sound, slashed
by light, hounded by a word. Go on,
even you who loved me. I can't keep up.
You were no match for my fantasies. Yes,
I should have saluted you as you passed,
but I was already busy getting over you.

Smoke

Is grievance to mind
as sap to leaf?
Without it leaf-mind
skitters in the smoke
to other kinds of life.

No grievance, no bloom,
yet I like fall and winter
and it doesn't follow
God's gift is grievance.
I don't need gravity

the way leaves need sap.
I notice grudges cling
long into blowhard snows,
ideologues preaching
to whitening choirs.

Fires of fall are banked
with swirling aspirations
to the whispered verges
whose password is let go.
Wind, I am light enough.

Even now the embers

And will I recognize you
on a playground or in a café
of the 13th world
where we will have gone
to sort this out again
and will I remember
how much I feared
not recognizing you

and why of all the lives we've lived
should this be the memorable one?

To whom do they belong,
these faces that we rent
to attend the ball,
and when the music stops
and we look around
who will we truly leave?
I am afraid each time
I will not find you again.

www.ingramcontent.com/pod-product-compliance
Lightning Source LLC
LaVergne TN
LVHW041548070426
835507LV00011B/991